Unlock Your Financial IQ to Open the Door to Financial Freedom

Unlock Your Financial IQ to Open the Door to Financial Freedom

Introduction to Powerful Financial Tools that Build Residual Income & Protects your Assets.

Quinn Harris

Quinn Harris
Unlock Your Financial IQ to Open the Door to Financial Freedom

Published by Spines

ISBN: 979-8-89569-816-7

Disclaimer

I am not a financial advisor, and this is not financial advice. It is important to note that any financial advice provided is for informational purposes only and should not be considered professional advice. It is advised that you should do your own research before investing. You also need to understand that investing, in general, involves risk, and you must never invest more than you are willing to lose. Always consult with a financial advisor before making any financial decisions.

Contents

Introduction

This book will educate you in order to increase your financial IQ and empower you to have an advantage over the financial industry. Giving you inside access to the most powerful financial tools as well as transparency to make an informed decision and instructions on how to set yourself up to achieve financial freedom to build generational wealth.

Acknowledgments

I extend my deepest gratitude to my Father, whose spiritual guidance and wisdom laid the foundation for this book. Giving me the special knowledge to empower others to enhance their financial IQ.

To my husband, your skepticism fueled my determination. Thank you for the unintended motivation.

To my readers, I acknowledge and appreciate those who will learn from, apply and take action based on the insights within these pages. May this book inspire positive change in achieving financial freedom.

Thank you.

Preface

The fastest way to achieve financial freedom is to take a leap of Faith… let go of fear by taking action.

Letting go of money and investing it, not spending it, and not always saving it because, according to the Money Bible, money must move as it is energy. Why is it called currency and liquidity? Because it is under the water law.

Invest in yourself by buying knowledge because you are your greatest asset and the best investment you will ever make.

Think big in order to develop the reality you want. Always remember that you are the artist of your life, so paint your own picture and don't allow anyone to ever take your paintbrush away.

If anyone attempts to stand in your way, kill them with kindness, slay them with a smile and murder them with a kiss.

Use your imagination and ideas to build financial freedom, and G❤️D will give it Life.

My Story

I was tired of working hard, living paycheck to paycheck and not having enough money and time to do what I love. I was tired of not having money, borrowing money and trying all the "get-rich" schemes only to make other people rich.

I was desperate and looking for answers, and then I was introduced to powerful financial tools that I had never heard of before. At first, I was skeptical but intrigued.

Thanks to the audiobooks "The Money Bible" and "The Power of Now," I made an informed decision to take a leap of faith by taking action and letting go of the fear of losing money. Meaning I reframed my mindset from fear to opportunity. I stopped spending money, as spending means to waste, and I began investing money into different financial tools, as investing means to grow.

I stopped saving money, as savers are losers if you're not putting money to work for you. Money must be invested in order to grow and multiply, as money is currency and liquidity, and it must move, not stay stagnant, meaning it is saved at a bank.

My financial tools of choice have transformed my finances. Money no longer controls me; I control it. I have unlocked my financial IQ and opened the door to financial freedom that allowed me to take my finances to the next level. Now I want for nothing.

A Promise To Myself

I will take responsibility and financially educate myself moving forward to pass down knowledge throughout generations in order to build generational wealth.

I was not taught financial literacy at home, and because of this, I struggled financially.

I did not learn financial literacy at school, and because of this, I lived paycheck to paycheck.

I will no longer struggle financially or live paycheck to paycheck because I will invest in educating myself and apply what I learn to my financial life.

In the past, I had shame and guilt (negative energy).

In the present, I live in the NOW (positive energy).

I refuse to discuss the past.

I refuse to allow shame and guilt to control my life.

I don't speak on negativity because I refuse to give it life.

What the mind thinks and the mouth speaks, the body follows.

I've learned how to unpack my shame and guilt suitcase forever.

This I call financial soul care.

Chapter 1

Balance Sheet Of My Life

Birth is my opening stock.
Death is a closing stock.
What comes to me is credit.
What goes from me is debit.
My friends are my assets.
My bad habits are my liabilities.
My health is my goodwill.
My soul is my fixed asset.
My happiness is my profit.
Sorrow is your loss.
My character is my capital.
My knowledge is my investment.
Age is your depreciation.
Always remember,
Karma is your auditor.
I will have a great balance sheet of my life.

Chapter 2

Poor Mindset Vs. Rich Mindset

POOR MINDSET

- Controlled by money.
- Work for money.
- Spend, don't invest.
- Fear of credit cards.
- Don't have multiple credit cards.
- Don't trade credit cards.
- Don't have creditation.
- Use cash over credit.
- Don't think outside the box.
- Rather earn than learn.
- Look at cost, not value.
- Buy liabilities.
- Don't invest money to make money.
- Work harder, not smarter.
- Employee mindset.
- Pay high taxes.

- Invest in low-end opportunities.
- Outside investors and consumers.
- Put money in a bank or under the mattress.
- Don't ask the right questions.
- Make statements 'I can't afford it'.

  * A statement closes the mind.

RICH MINDSET

- Not controlled by money.
- Don't work for money.
- Invest more than spend.
- No fear of credit cards.
- Have multiple credit cards.
- Trade credit cards.
- Have creditation.
- Use credit over cash.
- Think outside the box.
- Learn then earn.
- Look at value, not cost.
- Buy assets.
- Invest money to make money.
- Work smarter, not harder.
- Entrepreneur mindset.
- Avoid taxes.
- Invest in high-end opportunities.
- Are inside investors and owners.

- Put more money into investments or opportunities.
- Ask the right question.
- Ask questions, '"How can I afford it"?

* A question opens the mind.

Chapter 3
Introduction to Financial Literacy

Financial literacy refers to the ability to understand and manage personal finances effectively, making informed decisions about earning, saving, investing, and spending money. It includes knowledge of financial concepts, such as:

1. Budgeting and expense management.

2. Saving and emergency funds.

3. Debt management and credit management.

4. Investing and retirement planning.

5. Risk management and insurance.

6. Financial goal setting and planning.

7. Understanding financial markets and instruments.

8. Tax awareness and planning financial literacy skills enable individuals to:

1. Make informed financial decisions.
2. Avoid debt and financial pitfalls.
3. Build wealth and achieve financial stability.
4. Adapt to changing financial circumstances.
5. Improve overall financial well-being.

Promoting financial literacy is essential for individuals, communities, and societies to foster economic stability, reduce financial stress, and enhance overall quality of life.

Chapter 4
Who Needs Financial Literacy

Financial literacy is for everyone, regardless of age, income, or financial situation. It's essential for:

1. Individuals:

To manage personal finances, achieve financial stability, and reach long-term goals.

2. Students:

To understand financial basics, make informed decisions, and develop good financial habits.

3. Low-income households:

To manage limited resources, access affordable financial services, and break cycles of poverty.

4. Retirees:

To maximize retirement income, manage expenses, and maintain financial security.

5. Small business owners:

To manage cash flow, access capital, and grow their businesses.

6. Investors:

To make informed investment decisions, manage risk, and achieve financial goals.

7. Families:

To manage household finances, teach children about money, and achieve shared financial goals.

8. Communities:

To promote economic development, reduce financial inequality, and foster financial stability.

9. Employees:

To understand employee benefits, manage workplace financial programs, and achieve financial wellness.

10. Everyone:

To navigate the complex financial landscape, avoid financial pitfalls, and achieve financial well-being.

Financial literacy is a lifelong learning process, and it's essential for individuals to continuously update their knowledge and skills to adapt to changing financial circumstances.

Chapter 5
Financial Literacy 101

Here's a step-by-step guide to financial literacy:

Step 1: Set Financial Goals:

1. Identify short-term goals (less than 1 year).
2. Identify long-term goals (1-5 years or more).
3. Prioritize goals.

Step 2: Track Expenses:

1. Record every transaction for 1 month.
2. Categorize expenses (housing, food, transportation, etc.)
3. Identify areas for reduction.

Step 3: Create a Budget:

1. Allocate 50% of income towards necessities (housing, food, utilities).
2. Allocate 30% towards discretionary spending (entertainment, hobbies).
3. Allocate 20% towards saving and debt repayment.

Step 4: Manage Debt:

1. List all debts (credit cards, loans, etc.)
2. Prioritize high-interest debts.
3. Pay more than the minimum payment.
4. Consider debt consolidation or balance transfer.

Step 5: Build an Emergency Fund:

1. Save $1,000-$2,000.
2. Keep funds in a readily accessible savings account.
3. Avoid dipping into the fund for non-essentials.

Step 6: Invest for the Future:

1. Take advantage of employer-matched retirement accounts (401(k), IRA).
2. Consider other investment options (brokerage accounts, robo-advisors).
3. Start small and increase contributions over time.

Step 7: Monitor Credit Reports:

1. Request a free credit report from each major credit bureau (Experian, TransUnion, Equifax).
2. Review reports for errors or inaccuracies.
3. Dispute errors and work to improve credit score.

Step 8: Practice Long-Term Thinking:

1. Avoid impulse purchases.
2. Consider the long-term implications of financial decisions.
3. Prioritize needs over wants.

Step 9: Stay Educated:

1. Continuously learn about personal finance.
2. Stay up to date on changes in the financial landscape.
3. Seek professional advice when needed.

Step 10: Review and Adjust:

1. Regularly review financial progress.
2. Adjust budget, investments, and goals as needed.
3. Celebrate milestones and stay motivated.

Remember, financial literacy is a lifelong journey.

· · ·

By following these steps and staying committed, you'll be well on your way to achieving financial stability and success.

Chapter 6

Test your Financial IQ

Financial literacy quiz:

1. What is the 50/30/20 rule?

   a. Allocate 50% of income towards savings, 30% towards expenses, and 20% towards debt repayment.
   b. Allocate 50% of income towards expenses, 30% towards savings, and 20% towards debt repayment.
   c. Allocate 50% of income towards debt repayment, 30% towards savings, and 20% towards expenses.
   d. Allocate 50% of income towards savings, 30% towards debt repayment, and 20% towards expenses.

Answer: b) Allocate 50% of income towards expenses, 30% towards savings, and 20% towards debt repayment.

2. What is compound interest?

   a. Interest earned on both the principal amount and any accrued interest.
   b. Interest earned only on the principal amount.
   c. Interest earned only on accrued interest.
   d. No interest earned.

Answer: a) Interest earned on both the principal amount and any accrued interest.

3. What is a credit score?

   a. A measure of income level.
   b. A measure of creditworthiness.
   c. A measure of employment history.
   d. A measure of education level.

Answer: b) A measure of creditworthiness.

4. What is the main benefit of having an emergency fund?

   a. To invest in stocks.
   b. To pay off debt.
   c. To cover unexpected expenses.
   d. To increase income.

Answer: c) To cover unexpected expenses.

5. What is the difference between a need and a want?

a. A need is something you want, while a want is something you need.
b. A need is essential, while a want is discretionary.
c. A need is discretionary, while a want is essential.
d. There is no difference.

Answer: b) A need is essential, while a want is discretionary.

6. What is the main advantage of a high-yield savings account?

a. High returns on investment.
b. Low risk and liquidity.
c. Tax benefits.
d. Investment in stocks.

Answer: b) Low risk and liquidity.

7. Which of the following is a characteristic of a credit score?

a. Measures income level.
b. Measures creditworthiness.
c. Measures employment history.
d. Measures education level.

Answer: b) Measures creditworthiness.

8. What is the primary purpose of a budget?

    a. To track expenses.
    b. To increase income.
    c. To manage debt.
    d. To achieve financial goals.

Answer: d) To achieve financial goals.

9. Which investment option typically carries the highest level of risk?

    a. Stocks
    b. Bonds
    c. Mutual funds
    d. Savings account

Answer: a) Stocks

10. What is the benefit of paying off high-interest debt?

    a. Reduces monthly payments.
    b. Increases credit score.
    c. Saves money on interest.
    d. Increases income.

Answer: c) Saves money on interest.

11. What is the purpose of an emergency fund?

    a. To invest in stocks.
    b. To pay off debt.
    c. To cover unexpected expenses.
    d. To increase income.

Answer: c) To cover unexpected expenses.

12. Which of the following is a type of retirement account?

    a. 401(k)
    b. IRA
    c. Roth IRA
    d. All of the above

Answer: d) All of the above

13. What is the benefit of compound interest?

    a. Increases interest rates.
    b. Reduces interest rates.
    c. Increases investment returns over time.
    d. Decreases investment returns over time.

Answer: c) Increases investment returns over time.

14. Which of the following is a characteristic of a Roth IRA?

   a. Tax-deductible contributions.
   b. Tax-free withdrawals.
   c. Required minimum distributions.
   d. Income limits on contributions.

Answer: b) Tax-free withdrawals.

15. What is the purpose of a financial goal?

   a. To increase income.
   b. To reduce expenses.
   c. To achieve a specific financial outcome.
   d. To decrease debt.

Answer: c) To achieve a specific financial outcome.

Chapter 7

Credit Quiz

Choose the correct answer for each question.

1. What affects your credit score the most?

    A. Payment history
    B. Credit utilization
    C. Credit age
    D. Credit mix

A) Payment history

2. What is the ideal credit utilization ratio?

    A. 0-30%
    B. 31-50%
    C. 51-70%
    D. 71-100%

A) 0-30%

3. How often should you check your credit report?

A. Annually
B. Quarterly
C. Monthly
D. Daily

A) Annually

4. What can hurt your credit score?

A. On-time payments
B. Credit Inquiries
C. High credit limits
D. Low credit utilization

B) Credit inquiries

5. What type of credit is a mortgage?

A. Revolving credit
B. Installment credit
C. Open credit
D. Secured credit

B) Installment credit

6. How long does negative information stay on your credit report?

A. 1-2 years
B. 5-7 years
C. 10-15 years
D. Forever

B) 5-7 years

7. What is a good credit score range?

A. 600-649
B. 650-699
C. 700-749
D. 750-850

D) 750-850

8. Why should you avoid excessive credit applications?

A. High interest rates
B. Fees
C. Credit score impact
D. All of the above

C) Credit score impact

9. What benefits come with a good credit score?

A. Lower interest rates
B. Higher credit limits
C. Better loan terms
D. All of the above

D) All of the above

10. Who provides credit scores?

A. Banks
B. Credit bureaus
C. Government
D. Lenders

B) Credit bureaus

Credit bureaus Scoring:

1-3 correct answers: Credit beginner
4-6 correct answers: Credit intermediate
7-10 correct answers: Credit expert

Chapter 8
Financial Literacy Guide

Here's a step-by-step guide to financial literacy:

Step 1: Set Financial Goals:

1. Identify short-term goals (less than 1 year).
2. Identify long-term goals (1-5 years or more).
3. Prioritize goals.

Step 2: Track Expenses:

1. Record every transaction for 1 month.
2. Categorize expenses (housing, food, transportation, etc.)
3. Identify areas for reduction.

Step 3: Create a Budget:

1. Allocate 50% of income towards necessities (housing, food, utilities).
2. Allocate 30% towards discretionary spending (entertainment, hobbies).
3. Allocate 20% towards saving and debt repayment.

Step 4: Manage Debt:

1. List all debts (credit cards, loans, etc.)
2. Prioritize high-interest debts.
3. Pay more than the minimum payment.
4. Consider debt consolidation or balance transfer.

Step 5: Build an Emergency Fund:

1. Save $1,000-$2,000
2. Keep funds in a readily accessible savings account.
3. Avoid dipping into the fund for non-essentials.

Step 6: Invest for the Future:

1. Take advantage of employer-matched retirement accounts (401(k), IRA).
2. Consider other investment options (brokerage accounts, robo-advisors).
3. Start small and increase contributions over time.

Step 7: Monitor Credit Reports:

1. Request a free credit report from each major credit bureau (Experian, TransUnion, Equifax).
2. Review reports for errors or inaccuracies.
3. Dispute errors and work to improve credit score.

Step 8: Practice Long-Term Thinking:

1. Avoid impulse purchases.
2. Consider the long-term implications of financial decisions.
3. Prioritize needs over wants.

Step 9: Stay Educated:

1. Continuously learn about personal finance.
2. Stay up to date on changes in the financial landscape.
3. Seek professional advice when needed.

Step 10: Review and Adjust:

1. Regularly review financial progress.
2. Adjust budget, investments, and goals as needed.
3. Celebrate milestones and stay motivated.

Remember, financial literacy is a lifelong journey.

By following these steps and staying committed, you'll be well on your way to achieving financial stability and success.

Chapter 9

Financial Literacy According to Age

Step-by-step guide to financial literacy according to age:

Age 14-18:

1. Budgeting: Learn to manage your money and prioritize expenses.
2. Saving: Understand the importance of saving for short-term and long-term goals.
3. Credit and Debt: Learn about credit cards, loans, and responsible borrowing.
4. Earning: Explore ways to earn money, such as part-time jobs or entrepreneurship.
5. Financial Goals: Set and work towards achieving financial goals, like saving for college.

Age 19-25:

1. Financial Independence: Take responsibility for your financial decisions.
2. Investing: Learn about investment options, such as stocks, bonds, and ETFs.
3. Retirement Savings: Understand the importance of starting early with retirement savings.
4. Credit Score: Learn how credit scores work and how to maintain a good score.
5. Emergency Fund: Build an emergency fund to cover unexpected expenses.

Age 26-35:

1. Long-term Investing: Develop a long-term investment strategy.
2. Debt Management: Learn to manage debt, including student loans and mortgages.
3. Insurance: Understand the importance of insurance (health, auto, home).
4. Financial Planning: Create a comprehensive financial plan.
5. Tax Planning: Learn about tax-advantaged accounts and deductions.

Age 36-50:

1. Wealth Building: Focus on building wealth through investments and savings.
2. Retirement Planning: Develop a detailed retirement plan.
3. Estate Planning: Learn about wills, trusts, and estate planning.
4. Risk Management: Understand and manage financial risks.
5. Philanthropy: Consider giving back through charitable donations.

Age 51+:

1. Retirement Optimization: Maximize retirement income and benefits.
2. Legacy Planning: Plan to leave a legacy for your loved ones.
3. Long-term Care: Understand long-term care options and planning.
4. Investment Optimization: Refine your investment strategy.
5. Financial Legacy: Consider passing on financial knowledge to the next generation. Remember, financial literacy is a lifelong learning process. Start with the basics and build your knowledge over time.

Health is the real wealth. Stay rich... G❤️D B🙏

Chapter 10

The Wealth Builder Plan for Every Age

IN YOUR 20's

- Open checking and savings accounts if you don't have them.
- Deposit 5% of your salary into your savings account each period.
- Start an emergency fund with the goal of saving three to six month's pay.
- Take advantage of employee benefits including 401(k), 403(b), pension, health, and other insurance.
- Contribute at least the minimum percentage needed to qualify for the full employee match on the 401(k).
- If your company doesn't offer a 401(k), open an IRA. Then set up automatic contributions to the plan.

- Limit yourself to 1 credit card for emergencies and pay the balance each month.
- Learn to create a budget and stick to it.
- Work on paying down existing debt as quickly as possible - including student loans and credit cards. Start with the highest rate of debt.
- Check your credit report for discrepancies. Obtain a baseline credit score and make adjustments if necessary.
- Lock in a low rate on your life insurance and disability income insurance.

NOTES

IN YOUR 30's

- Continue contributing to your 401(k) plan or IRA. Aim for 10% of your paycheck.
- Invest in your 401(k) Plan or IRA money more aggressively (stock-based mutual funds) to keep pace with inflation.
- Put a 20% down payment on a home purchase to avoid the cost of mortgage insurance. Your mortgage payment should be no more than 28% of your monthly income (based on lender guidelines).
- Get a Prenup, Will, Trust, and Life Insurance Policy to protect your assets.

NOTES

IN YOUR 50's

- Revisit your retirement savings goal to make sure it still makes sense.
- Do the math - add up how much retirement income you expect to receive, then see how much you think you need. If there's an income gap (you need more than you have), address it now.
- If you're behind on savings, you can catch up by taking advantage of higher contribution limits in 401(k)s and IRAs.
- Consider a deferred annuity as an option in your savings/investment plans.
- Review your estate plan to make sure it is up to date with changes in your life and current laws. Confirm that executors and guardians are still properly chosen.
- Re-evaluate your 401(k) or IRA investment mix to ensure it meets your planned retirement date.
- Review your total Insurance protection. Consider adding a long-term care policy.

NOTES

IN YOUR 60's

- Review your retirement income strategy. Determine whether you can live off a small percentage of your retirement assets and continue investing the majority or if you need to begin receiving an income stream. Continue to invest your retirement assets if you don't need them for income.
- Think about choices that may reduce your essential expenses in retirement without compromising what's important to you. For example, will you retire where you live now or move to someplace that might reduce your cost of living?

NOTES

Chapter 11

What is a Bank

A bank is a financial institution that provides a wide range of financial services to individuals, businesses, and governments.

Some of the main functions of a bank include:

1. Accepting deposits: Banks allow customers to deposit money into their accounts, which can earn interest.
2. Making loans: Banks lend money to customers for various purposes, such as buying a home, starting a business, or financing education.
3. Providing payment services: Banks facilitate transactions, such as checking and savings accounts, credit cards, and electronic payments.
4. Managing risk: Banks offer insurance and

investment products to help customers manage risk.

5. Facilitating international trade: Banks provide services for international trade, such as foreign exchange and letters of credit.
6. Offering investment products: Banks provide investment advice and products, such as mutual funds and stocks.
7. Providing credit cards and debit cards: Banks issue credit and debit cards, allowing customers to make purchases and access cash.
8. Offering mortgage services: Banks provide mortgage loans and refinancing options for homeowners.
9. Providing online and mobile banking: Banks offer digital platforms for customers to manage their accounts and conduct transactions.
10. Maintaining financial stability: Banks play a crucial role in maintaining financial stability by managing risk, regulating transactions, and providing liquidity.

Banks can be categorized into different types, including:

1. Retail banks
2. Commercial banks
3. Investment banks
4. Central banks
5. Community banks
6. Online banks

Each type of bank has its unique features and services, but they all share the common goal of facilitating financial transactions and providing financial services to their customers.

Chapter 12

Pros and Cons of Putting Money in a Bank

Airy pros and cons of conventional banking or putting your money in a bank:

Pros:

1. Liquidity: Easy access to your money through ATMs, online banking, and branch withdrawals.
2. Security: Deposits are insured up to a certain amount (e.g., $250,000 in the US), protecting your money.
3. Convenience: Wide range of services, including bill pay, transfers, and credit cards.
4. Low risk: Banks are generally considered a low-risk place to store your money.
5. Interest earnings: You can earn interest on your deposits, although rates are typically low.
6. Branch and ATM network: Access to a large network of branches and ATMs.

7. Financial management tools: Many banks offer online tools to help manage your finances.

Cons:

1. Low interest rates: Interest rates on deposits are often lower than inflation, reducing purchasing power.
2. Fees and charges: Banks charge various fees, such as overdraft, maintenance, and ATM fees.
3. Inflation risk: Inflation can erode the purchasing power of your money over time.
4. Credit risk: Although rare, banks can fail, putting your deposits at risk.
5. Limited control: You have limited control over how your money is used or invested.
6. Dependence on banks: You rely on banks for financial services, which can be inconvenient if they experience outages or issues.
7. Potential for negative interest rates: In some cases, banks may charge negative interest rates, reducing your deposits.

Remember, conventional banking is a traditional and widely used option for managing your finances. However, it's essential to be aware of the pros and cons and consider alternative options, such as investing or alternative banking solutions, to find the best fit for your financial goals and needs.

Chapter 13

How to Set Up the Best Bank Account

Setting up the best bank account for your needs involves considering several factors. Here's a step-by-step guide:

Determine Your Banking Needs:

1. Personal or business use
2. Frequency of transactions
3. Minimum balance requirements
4. Interest earnings
5. Fees (maintenance, overdraft, ATM)
6. Online banking and mobile app accessibility
7. Customer support
8. Security features

Types of Bank Accounts:

1. Checking accounts
2. Savings accounts
3. Money market accounts
4. High-yield savings accounts
5. Certificates of Deposit (CDs)
6. Business checking accounts

Best Bank Account Features:

1. No monthly maintenance fees.
2. No overdraft fees.
3. High-interest rates (for savings accounts).
4. Low or no minimum balance requirements.
5. ATM fee reimbursement.
6. Mobile deposit and online bill pay.
7. Budgeting and financial management tools.
8. Two-factor authentication and fraud protection.

Top Banks and Credit Unions:

1. National banks:

- Chase Bank
- Bank of America
- Wells Fargo
- Citi Bank

2. Online banks:

- Ally Bank
- Capital One 360
- Discover Bank
- Marcus by Goldman Sachs

3. Credit unions:

- Navy Federal Credit Union
- Alliant Credit Union
- PenFed Credit Union

Setting Up Your Bank Account:

1. Visit the bank's website or branch.
2. Provide required documents (ID, SSN, proof of address).
3. Fill out the application.
4. Fund the account (initial deposit).
5. Set up online banking and mobile app access.
6. Review and sign account agreements.

Digital Banking Platforms:

1. Chime Bank
2. Simple Bank
3. Varo Bank
4. Digit Bank
5. Current Bank

Considerations for Specific Needs:

1. Students: Look for student-friendly accounts with no fees.
2. Small business owners: Consider business checking accounts with low fees.
3. International travelers: Choose accounts with no foreign transaction fees.
4. High-income earners: Explore premium accounts with high interest rates.

Final Check:

1. Review account terms and conditions.
2. Understand fees and charges.
3. Verify customer support options.
4. Ensure mobile app and online banking functionality.

By following these steps, you'll find the best bank account tailored to your financial needs.

Chapter 14
What the Banking System Might not Want You to Know

Here are some things the banking system might not want you to know:

1. Fees are a major profit source: Banks charge various fees, such as overdraft, ATM, and maintenance fees, which can be lucrative.
2. Low interest rates on deposits: Banks pay minimal interest on deposits while charging high interest on loans and credit cards.
3. Credit scoring manipulation: Banks influence credit scoring models to control who gets credit and at what interest rate.
4. Overdraft fee traps: Banks may reorder transactions to maximize overdraft fees.
5. NSF fee abuse: Banks charge high fees for non-sufficient funds, even if the overdraft is small.
6. Banking for the wealthy: Banks often prioritize

     services and products for high-net-worth individuals.

7. Systemic risk-taking: Banks engage in risky practices, putting the financial system at risk.
8. Lobbying and regulatory influence: Banks exert significant influence over financial regulations and laws.
9. Data mining and privacy concerns: Banks collect and profit from customer data.
10. Alternative banking options: Banks might not want you to know about alternative banking options, such as credit unions or fintech companies.
11. Inflation and currency devaluation: Banks benefit from inflation and currency devaluation, which can erode savings.
12. Bail-in risks: In the event of a bank failure, depositors may be subject to "bail-in" measures, converting deposits into bank equity.
13. Fractional reserve banking: Banks create new money by lending, which can lead to economic instability.
14. Derivatives and hidden risks: Banks engage in complex derivatives trading, posing hidden risks to the financial system.

Remember to stay informed and vigilant about banking practices to protect your financial interests.

Chapter 15

What the Bank Representative Might not Want You to Know

Here are some additional things banks might not want you to know:

1. You don't have to keep all your accounts at one bank: Spread your accounts to minimize risk and maximize benefits.
2. Banking services are often unnecessary: Be cautious of add-on services like overdraft protection or credit monitoring.
3. Credit unions and community banks are alternatives: Consider these options for better rates and personalized service.
4. You can negotiate fees and rates: Ask your bank to waive fees or offer better rates, especially if you're a loyal customer.
5. Banks sell your data: Be aware of how your data is used and consider opting out of data sharing.

6. There are alternative payment methods: Consider digital wallets, cryptocurrencies, or peer-to-peer payment apps.
7. Banks may not be FDIC-insured: Verify your bank's insurance status to ensure your deposits are protected.
8. You can take control of your finances: Educate yourself on personal finance and consider DIY banking solutions.
9. Banks have conflicts of interest: Be aware of potential biases in banking advice or product recommendations.
10. Technology can replace traditional banking: Explore fintech options for more efficient and cost-effective banking.

Remember, knowledge is power. Stay informed and take control of your financial life!

Chapter 16

Powerful Financial Tools Summary

VELOCITY BANKING SUMMARY

Velocity Banking is a financial strategy that optimizes mortgage payments and credit utilization to minimize interest expenses and maximize wealth.

INFINITE BANKING CONCEPT SUMMARY

Infinite Banking is a financial strategy that utilizes whole life insurance policies to build wealth and create a personalized banking system.

CREDIT STACKING SYSTEM

Credit Stacking is a financial strategy that leverages credit cards' rewards, benefits and promotional offers to generate wealth.

Chapter 17

The Most Powerful Financial Tool

Credit Card Trading:

The art and science of combining all three strategies (Velocity, Infinite and Credit Stacking) with a patent signature twist. Want to afford anything?

Let B.Pro show you how.

Visit: creditcardtrading.com

Quinn Harris
(845) 502-6529

Chapter 18

Velocity Banking with a HELOC

Velocity banking is a financial strategy that uses a home equity line of credit (HELOC) to accelerate mortgage payoff and reduce interest expenses:

- Set up a HELOC, which acts as your primary checking account.
- Deposit your paycheck into the HELOC, reducing the principal balance and interest charges.
- Use the HELOC to pay monthly bills and living expenses, keeping the balance low.
- Periodically, use the HELOC to make a large payment toward your primary mortgage or other significant debts.
- Repeat the cycle, continually reducing the principal on larger loans and saving on interest.

The benefits of velocity banking include:

- Faster debt payoff
- Significant interest savings
- Enhanced financial flexibility
- Empowerment and control over debts

However, risks and challenges associated with velocity banking include:

- Financial discipline is required.
- Variable interest rates may increase.
- Dependence on consistent income.
- Over-reliance on property value.
- Potential for overspending.

It's essential to understand the terms of your HELOC, stay disciplined with spending, and regularly review and adjust your strategy as needed.

Chapter 19

Pros & Cons of Velocity Banking with a HELOC

(Home Equity Line of Credit) involves using a HELOC to accelerate debt repayment, optimize cash flow, and build wealth. Here are the pros and cons:

Pros:

1. Debt elimination: Accelerate paying off high-interest debts (e.g., credit cards, personal loans).
2. Cash flow optimization: Use HELOC funds to cover expenses, reducing the need for other debt.
3. Wealth growth: Invest HELOC funds in high-return assets (e.g., stocks, real estate).
4. Tax benefits: Potential tax deductions on HELOC interest.
5. Flexibility: Access funds as needed, repay, and re-borrow.

6. Low interest rates: HELOC rates are often lower than credit card rates.
7. Consolidation: Combine multiple debts into one manageable loan.

Cons:

1. Risk of overspending: Easy access to funds can lead to overspending.
2. Variable interest rates: HELOC rates may increase, affecting repayment.
3. Fees: Origination fees, annual fees, and closing costs.
4. Collateral risk: Your home serves as collateral, risking foreclosure.
5. Repayment pressure: Required monthly payments can be stressful.
6. Credit score impact: Missed payments or high credit utilization harm credit scores.
7. Market volatility: Investing HELOC funds in volatile markets risks losses.

Additional Considerations:

1. HELOC terms: Understand interest rates, fees, and repayment terms.
2. Credit requirements: Typically requires good credit (700+ FICO score).
3. Debt-to-income ratio: Ensure you can manage HELOC payments.
4. Financial discipline: Essential for successful Velocity Banking.
5. Alternative strategies: Compare with other debt consolidation methods.

Best Suited For:

1. Disciplined individuals with stable income.
2. Those with high-interest debt and sufficient home equity.
3. Investors seeking low-interest funding for investments.
4. Homeowners with a clear financial plan.

Not Recommended For:

1. Those with poor credit or high debt-to-income ratios.
2. Individuals are prone to overspending.
3. Those without a stable income or emergency fund.
4. Homeowners with insufficient equity.

To mitigate risks, consider:

1. Setting a budget and sticking to it.
2. Regularly reviewing and adjusting your financial plan.
3. Building an emergency fund.
4. Consulting with a financial advisor.

By understanding the pros and cons, you can make an informed decision about using a HELOC for Velocity Banking.

Chapter 20

How to Set Up Velocity Banking With a HELOC

Velocity Banking is a debt-elimination strategy that leverages home equity to accelerate debt payoff. Here's a simplified, step-by-step guide:

Step 1: Prepare:

1. Gather financial documents:

- Mortgage statement
- Debt statements (credit cards, loans)
- Income verification
- Credit report

2. Calculate your debt-to-income ratio.
3. Determine your financial goals.

Step 2: Set Up Velocity Banking Accounts:

1. Open a:

- Primary checking account.
- Home equity line of credit (HELOC).
- Separate savings account (optional).

2. Ensure HELOC:

- Has a low interest rate.
- Has a sufficient credit limit.
- Allows for easy access (e.g., check writing, online transfers).

Step 3: Consolidate Debt:

1. Transfer high-interest debt to HELOC:

- Credit cards
- Personal loans
- Other high-interest debt

2. Leave low-interest debt (e.g., mortgage, student loans) unchanged.

Step 4: Create a Velocity Banking Cycle:

1. Deposit income into primary checking.
2. Transfer excess funds to HELOC.
3. Use HELOC to pay off debt.
4. Repeat the cycle monthly.

Step 5: Optimize and Accelerate:

1. Apply extra payments to the principal.
2. Consider bi-weekly payments.
3. Use a savings account for emergency funds.
4. Monitor and adjust strategy as needed.

Example:

- $200,000 mortgage @ 4% interest.
- $50,000 HELOC @ 3.5% interest.
- $20,000 credit card debt @ 18% interest.
- Monthly income: $5,000

1. Consolidate credit card debt to HELOC.
2. Deposit $5,000 in income into primary checking.
3. Transfer $2,000 excess to HELOC.
4. Use HELOC to pay off debt.
5. Repeat the cycle monthly.

Benefits:

1. Reduced debt payoff time
2. Lower interest rates
3. Increased cash flow
4. Improved credit score

Risks and Considerations:

1. HELOC interest rates may fluctuate.
2. Debt consolidation may not address underlying spending habits.
3. Credit score impact
4. Risk of overspending

Professional Guidance:

Consult with a financial advisor or mortgage professional to ensure Velocity Banking is suitable for your situation.

Remember, Velocity Banking requires discipline and commitment. Stick to your plan and monitor progress to achieve financial freedom.

Chapter 21

Velocity Banking With a Credit Card

Velocity Banking with a credit card involves using a credit card strategically to optimize cash flow, reduce debt, and increase savings. Here's a detailed overview:

Key Principles:

1. Choose a credit card with:

- 0% introductory APR (12-18 months)
- No annual fee
- High credit limit

2. Use the credit card for:

- Essential expenses (e.g., groceries, utilities)
- Debt consolidation (e.g., paying off high-interest loans)
- Strategic purchases (e.g., large expenses, business investments)

3. Pay off the credit card balance in full each month or:

- Make multiple payments throughout the month.
- Use the snowball or avalanche method to pay off principal balances.

4. Take advantage of:

- 0% APR to avoid interest charges.
- Cashback, rewards, or sign-up bonuses.
- Credit limit increases to enhance cash flow.

Velocity Banking Strategies:

1. Debt Snowball: Pay off high-interest debts using a credit card.
2. Debt Avalanche: Prioritize debts with the highest interest rates.
3. Cash Flow Optimization: Use the credit card for expenses and pay off with incoming funds.
4. Mortgage Acceleration: Use the credit card to make extra mortgage payments.

Benefits:

1. Reduced debt
2. Increased cash flow
3. Improved credit utilization
4. Enhanced credit score
5. Increased savings through rewards and interest avoidance.

Risks:

1. Overspending
2. Interest charges, if not paid off in full
3. Fees (e.g., late fees, balance transfer fees)
4. Credit score impact if not managed properly.

Best Practices:

1. Set clear financial goals.
2. Monitor credit utilization (keep below 30%)
3. Make timely payments
4. Avoid overspending
5. Review and adjust strategies regularly.

Recommended Credit Cards:

1. Citi Double Cash Card
2. Chase Freedom Unlimited
3. Discover it Cash Back.
4. American Express Blue Cash Preferred
5. Capital One Quicksilver Cash Rewards

Important Note: Velocity Banking with a credit card requires discipline, organization, and financial awareness. Ensure you understand the terms and conditions of your credit card and manage your finances responsibly.

Chapter 22

Pros & Cons of Velocity Banking with a Credit Card.

Pros:

1. Accelerated debt repayment: By using a credit card to pay off high-interest debts or mortgages, you can potentially save thousands in interest.
2. Improved cash flow: Velocity banking allows you to manage cash flow more effectively, ensuring you have funds available when needed.
3. Increased liquidity: Credit cards provide access to additional funds for emergency expenses or investments.
4. Rewards and benefits: Earn rewards, such as cashback, points, or travel benefits, on purchases.
5. Simplified financial management: Consolidate debts and manage payments through a single credit card account.

6. Potential interest savings: By paying off debts quickly, you can reduce interest paid over time.

Cons:

1. Risk of overspending: Using a credit card for velocity banking requires discipline to avoid overspending.
2. Interest charges: If not paid off in full each month, interest charges can negate benefits.
3. Fees: Credit cards may have annual fees, late fees, or balance transfer fees.
4. Credit score impact: Missed payments or high credit utilization can harm credit scores.
5. Complexity: Velocity banking strategies can be complex and difficult to manage.
6. Dependence on credit: Relying on credit cards for cash flow management can create dependence.
7. Risk of credit limit reductions: Credit card issuers may reduce limits, impacting velocity banking strategies.
8. Potential for debt accumulation: If not executed correctly, velocity banking can lead to increased debt.

To mitigate risks:

1. Set clear financial goals and strategies.
2. Maintain a budget and track expenses.
3. Pay off credit card balances in full each month.
4. Monitor credit utilization and scores.
5. Avoid overspending and impulse purchases.
6. Consider consulting a financial advisor.

Chapter 23

How to Set Up Velocity Banking With a Credit Card

Setting up Velocity Banking with a credit card requires strategy and discipline. Here's a simplified, step-by-step guide:

Warning: This method involves using a credit card responsibly and paying off the balance in full each month.

Prerequisites:

1. Good credit score (700+)
2. Low-interest credit card (0% APR or low-interest rate)
3. Stable income
4. Financial discipline

Step-by-Step Setup:

Month 1-3: Preparation:

1. Choose a credit card:

- 0% APR promotional period (12-18 months)
- Low interest rate after the promotional period
- No annual fee

2. Set up automatic payments:

- Pay off the full balance each month.
- Ensure timely payments.

3. Monitor credit limit:

- Ensure sufficient credit limit for expenses.

Month 4-6: Debt Consolidation:

1. Consolidate high-interest debt:

- Transfer high-interest debt to a credit card.
- Leave low-interest debt unchanged.

2. Create a debt repayment plan:

- Prioritize high-interest debt.
- Allocate funds for debt repayment.

Velocity Banking Cycle:

1. Charge expenses to credit card:

- Daily expenses
- Bills
- Debt repayment

2. Receive rewards and cashback:

- Earn rewards on purchases.
- Redeem rewards for statement credits.

3. Pay off credit card balance:

- In full each month.
- Before interest charges apply.

4. Repeat cycle monthly:

Optimization Strategies:

1. Use credit card rewards:

- Cashback
- Travel rewards
- Statement credits

2. Take advantage of 0% APR:

- Transfer high-interest debt.
- Avoid interest charges.

3. Monitor credit utilization:

- Keep utilization below 30%
- Maintain a good credit score.

Example:

- Credit card: 0% APR for 12 months, $5,000 credit limit.
- Monthly expenses: $2,000
- High-interest debt: $10,000 @ 18% interest.
- Monthly debt repayment: $1,000

1. Consolidate high-interest debt to credit cards.
2. Charge monthly expenses to a credit card.
3. Receive rewards and cashback.
4. Pay off your credit card balance in full each month.
5. Repeat the cycle monthly.

Benefits:

1. Reduced debt payoff time
2. Lower interest rates
3. Increased cash flow
4. Improved credit score

Risks and Considerations:

1. Interest rate changes
2. Credit limit reductions
3. Overspending
4. Late payments

Professional Guidance:

Consult with a financial advisor to ensure Velocity Banking with a credit card is suitable for your situation.

Jason Nightingale, Velocity Banking Expert.

Remember, Velocity Banking with a credit card requires discipline and responsibility. Stick to your plan and monitor progress to achieve financial freedom.

Chapter 24

Velocity Banking Strategies

1. Debt snowball: Pay off high-interest debts using credit card funds.
2. Debt avalanche: Prioritize debts with the highest interest rates.
3. Cash flow optimization: Use credit cards for expenses and pay off with incoming funds.
4. Mortgage acceleration: Use credit cards to make extra mortgage payments.

Important note: Velocity banking with a credit card requires careful planning, discipline, and ongoing monitoring. It's essential to understand the terms and conditions of your credit card and ensure this strategy aligns with your financial goals and risk tolerance.

Velocity banking is a debt reduction strategy that involves aggressively paying off debts with high interest rates or high balances. Here's a step-by-step guide to set up velocity banking:

Pre-requisites:

1. Gather all financial documents, including debt statements, income proof, and budget details.
2. Create a budget that allocates a significant portion towards debt repayment.
3. Prioritize debts based on interest rates, balances, or urgency.

Velocity Banking Steps:

1. List all debts: Write down each debt, including balance, interest rate, minimum payment, and due date.

2. Categorize debts: Group debts into three categories:

- High-interest debts (e.g., credit cards)
- High-balance debts (e.g., mortgages, personal loans)
- Low-interest debts (e.g., student loans, mortgages)

3. Determine the velocity banking order: Prioritize debts using one of the following methods:

- Debt Snowball: Pay off debts with the smallest balances first.
- Debt Avalanche: Pay off debts with the highest interest rates first.
- Hybrid: Combine both methods, paying off high-interest debts with small balances first.

4. Calculate the total monthly payment: Allocate a fixed amount for debt repayment each month.

5. Assign payments: Allocate the total monthly payment among debts, focusing on the priority debt.

6. Pay more than the minimum: Pay as much as possible towards the priority debt.

7. Use the "waterfall" method: Once a debt is paid off, redirect the payment amount to the next priority debt.

8. Monitor progress: Regularly review the debt list and adjust the payment plan as needed.

Additional Strategies:

1. Consolidate debts: Combine multiple debts into a single, lower-interest loan.
2. Negotiate interest rates: Contact creditors to reduce interest rates or waive fees.
3. Use windfalls: Apply unexpected funds (e.g., tax refunds, bonuses) towards debt repayment.
4. Automate payments: Set up automatic transfers for debt payments.

Tools and Resources:

1. Spreadsheets (e.g., Google Sheets, Microsoft Excel)
2. Budgeting software (e.g., Mint, You Need a Budget)
3. Debt repayment apps (e.g., Debt Snowball, Payoff)
4. Financial advisors or credit counselors

Example:

Suppose you have the following debts:

Debt	Balance	Interest Rate	Minimum Payment
Credit Card	$2,000	18%	$50
Car Loan	$10,000	6%	$200

| Student Loan | $30,000 | 4% | $100 |

You allocate $1,000/month for debt repayment. You prioritize the credit card debt using the debt avalanche method.

| Month | Credit Card Payment | Car Loan Payment | Student Loan Payment |

| --- | --- | --- | --- |

| 1-6 | $1,000 | $0 | $0 |

| 7-12 | $500 | $500 | $0 |

| 13-24 | $0 | $1,000 | $0 |

| 25-60 | $0 | $0 | $1,000 |

By following these steps and strategies, you can accelerate your debt repayment and achieve financial freedom using Velocity banking.

Chapter 25
Infinite Banking

Setting up the best bank account for your needs involves considering several factors. Here's a step-by-step guide:

Determine Your Banking Needs:

1. Personal or business use

2. Frequency of transactions

3. Minimum balance requirements

4. Interest earnings

5. Fees (maintenance, overdraft, ATM)

6. Online banking and mobile app accessibility

7. Customer support

8. Security features

Types of Bank Accounts:

1. Checking accounts

2. Savings accounts

3. Money market accounts

4. High-yield savings accounts

5. Certificates of Deposit (CDs)

6. Business checking accounts

Best Bank Account Features:

1. No monthly maintenance fees

2. No overdraft fees

3. High-interest rates (for savings accounts)

4. Low or no minimum balance requirements

5. ATM fee reimbursement

6. Mobile deposit and online bill pay

7. Budgeting and financial management tools

8. Two-factor authentication and fraud protection

Top Banks and Credit Unions:

1. National banks:

- Chase Bank
- Bank of America
- Wells Fargo
- Citi Bank

2. Online banks:

- Ally Bank
- Capital One 360
- Discover Bank
- Marcus by Goldman Sachs

3. Credit unions:

- Navy Federal Credit Union
- Alliant Credit Union
- PenFed Credit Union

Setting Up Your Bank Account:

1. Visit the bank's website or branch

2. Provide required documents (ID, SSN, proof of address)

3. Fill out the application

4. Fund the account (initial deposit)

5. Set up online banking and mobile app access

6. Review and sign account agreements

Digital Banking Platforms:

1. Chime Bank

2. Simple Bank

3. Varo Bank

4. Digit Bank

5. Current Bank

Considerations for Specific Needs:

1. Students: Look for student-friendly accounts with no fees.
2. Small business owners: Consider business checking accounts with low fees.
3. International travelers: Choose accounts with no foreign transaction fees.
4. High-income earners: Explore premium accounts with high interest rates.

Final Check:

1. Review account terms and conditions.

2. Understand fees and charges.

3. Verify customer support options.

4. Ensure mobile app and online banking functionality.

By following these steps, you'll find the best bank account tailored to your financial needs.

Put Infinite Banking after Velocity Banking Strategy.

Before Pros and cons of infinite Banking.

Chapter 26

Pros & Cons of Infinite Banking

Pros:

1. Tax-Free Growth: The cash value of the policy grows tax-free.
2. Tax-Free Withdrawals: Policy loans and withdrawals are tax-free.
3. Guaranteed Returns: Whole life insurance policies typically offer guaranteed minimum returns.
4. Liquidity: Policy owners can access cash values through loans or withdrawals.
5. Dividend Potential: Many whole-life policies pay dividends, increasing policy values.
6. Asset Protection: Life insurance policies are often protected from creditors.
7. Estate Planning: Infinite Banking can be used to transfer wealth to heirs tax-free.

8. Retirement Income: Policy owners can use policy loans or withdrawals to supplement retirement income.
9. Business Funding: Infinite Banking can provide access to capital for business owners.
10. Financial Independence: By controlling your financial destiny, you can achieve financial independence.

Cons:

1. Complexity: Infinite Banking requires a sophisticated understanding of insurance and finance.
2. High Premiums: Whole life insurance policies can be expensive.
3. Surrender Charges: Early policy surrender can result in significant fees.
4. Interest Rates: Policy loan interest rates can be high.
5. Opportunity Cost: Tying up funds in a life insurance policy may limit other investment opportunities.
6. Lack of Flexibility: Policy terms and conditions can be inflexible.
7. Credit Risk: Borrowing from your policy can impact creditworthiness.
8. Administrative Costs: Policy administration fees can reduce returns.

9. Regulatory Risks: Changes in tax laws or regulations can impact policy benefits.
10. Agent Commissions: Buying a policy often involves paying agent commissions.

Additional Considerations:

1. Policy Design: The policy must be specifically designed for Infinite Banking.
2. Insurer Stability: Choose an insurer with a strong financial rating.
3. Cost of Insurance: Understand the cost of insurance charges.
4. Riders and Add-ons: Carefully evaluate additional policy features.

Chapter 27

How to Set Up Infinite Banking

To successfully implement Infinite Banking, it's essential to:

1. Consult with a qualified insurance professional.
2. Carefully evaluate policy terms and conditions.
3. Understand the fees and charges associated with the policy.
4. Monitor and adjust your policy as needed.

Infinite Banking can be a powerful financial tool, but it's crucial to weigh the pros and cons and consider individual circumstances before implementing this strategy.

Pre-requisites:

1. Understand the concept: Study the Infinite Banking concept, developed by Nelson Nash, to grasp its principles and benefits.
2. Financial stability: Ensure you have a stable income, manageable debt, and an emergency fund.
3. Long-term commitment: Infinite Banking requires a long-term commitment (10+ years).

Step 1: Choose the Right Life Insurance Policy:

1. Select a whole life insurance policy from a mutual insurance company (e.g., Northwestern Mutual, New York Life).
2. Look for policies with:

- High cash value accumulation potential.
- Low or no surrender charges.
- Dividend payments (participating policies).
- Flexible premium payment options.

Step 2: Design the Policy:

1. Determine the face value: Choose a face value that aligns with your financial goals.
2. Set the premium: Select a premium payment structure that fits your budget.
3. Riders and add-ons: Consider adding riders for increased flexibility (e.g., paid-up additions, term riders).

Step 3: Fund the Policy:

1. 1 Initial premium: Pay the initial premium to establish the policy.
2. Ongoing premiums: Pay premiums regularly to fund the policy.
3. Additional funding: Consider adding extra funds to the policy through paid-up additions or lump sums.

Step 4: Build Cash Value:

1. Allow the policy to accumulate cash value over time.
2. Monitor and adjust: Review policy performance and adjust premium payments or funding as needed.

Step 5: Use the Policy's Cash Value:

1. Loans: Borrow against the policy's cash value at favorable interest rates.
2. Withdrawals: Take tax-free withdrawals from the policy's cash value (after loans are repaid).
3. Dividend payments: Receive dividend payments from the insurance company.

Step 6: Review and Adjust:

1. Regular reviews: Monitor policy performance and adjust funding or loans as needed.
2. Tax implications: Consult with a tax professional to optimize tax benefits.

Important Considerations:

1. Fees and commissions: Understand the fees and commissions associated with the policy.
2. Insurance company stability: Research the insurance company's financial stability.
3. Policy complexity: Infinite Banking policies can be complex; seek professional guidance.
4. Regulatory compliance: Ensure compliance with insurance regulations and tax laws.

Professional Guidance:

To ensure successful implementation, consider consulting:

1. Licensed insurance professional.
2. Financial advisor experienced in Infinite Banking.
3. Tax professional.

Remember, Infinite Banking requires patience, discipline, and a long-term perspective. Proper setup and ongoing management are crucial to achieving its benefits.

Chapter 28

Financial Matrix

In finance, the "Red Pill" and "Blue Pill" analogy is borrowed from the 1999 film "The Matrix." It represents a choice between two different perspectives or approaches:

BLUE PILL:

1. Conventional wisdom
2. Mainstream investing
3. Following the crowd
4. Accepting the status quo
5. Investing in traditional assets (e.g., stocks, bonds)

RED PILL:

1. Unconventional wisdom
2. Alternative Investing
3. Challenging the status quo
4. Seeking truth and transparency
5. Investing in non-traditional assets (e.g., cryptocurrencies, precious metals)

In finance, taking the "red pill" means being open to new ideas, questioning established norms, and potentially taking on more risk.

It can lead to:

1. Higher potential returns
2. Greater control over investments
3. Increased transparency
4. Diversification
5. Potential for innovation

However, it also comes with:

1. Higher risk
2. Uncertainty
3. Potential for losses
4. Regulatory uncertainty
5. Social stigma

Taking the "blue pill" means following established norms, avoiding risk, and potentially missing out on alternative opportunities.

This analogy is often used in finance to describe the choice between:

1. Traditional investing vs. alternative investing.
2. Mainstream financial media vs. independent research.
3. Conventional wisdom vs. critical thinking.

Remember, this analogy is a metaphor, and it's essential to approach financial decisions with a clear understanding of your goals, risk tolerance, and the potential consequences of your choices.

Chapter 29
Person Stacking

Person Stacking, also known as "Personal Stacking" or "Entity Stacking," is a financial strategy that involves creating multiple entities or accounts in an individual's name to maximize financial benefits, reduce risk, and increase credit capacity.

Types of Persons Stacking:

1. Credit Card Stacking: Applying for multiple credit cards to maximize rewards, bonuses, and credit limits.
2. Bank Account Stacking: Opening multiple bank accounts to earn higher interest rates, reduce fees, and increase FDIC insurance coverage.
3. Entity Stacking: Creating multiple business entities (e.g., LLCs, trusts) to separate finances, reduce liability, and increase credit capacity.

4. Identity Stacking: Using variations of one's name (e.g., initials, middle names) to create multiple credit profiles.

Benefits:

1. Increased credit capacity

2. Improved credit utilization

3. Enhanced financial flexibility

4. Reduced risk through diversification

5. Increased rewards and bonuses

6. Improved interest earnings

7. Better financial organization

Risks and Considerations:

1. Credit inquiries and applications

2. Identity theft and credit monitoring

3. Overdraft risks

4. Fee management

5. Tax implications

6. Complexity and management

7. Regulatory compliance

Chapter 30
Credit Card Trading

Credit Card Trading is setting up a private bank within the credit card system, incorporating Velocity Banking, Infinite Banking and Credit Stacking. A gateway to financial freedom and generational wealth.

IMAGINE TRADING outside of the stock market, trading bad debt for good debt, using powerful financial tools.

Chapter 31

Stock Trading vs Credit Card Trading

Stock Trading

- Open a brokerage account.
- Education
- Buy the right investment with your money.
- Buy and sell
- Trade daily
- Trades are limited
- Taxed on gains
- Gains reported to the IRS.
- Rules to follow

Credit Card Trading

- Have a good credit score.
- Creditation (Steps to follow)
- Buy assets with other people's money (OPM)
- Receive credits
- Multiple credit cards
- Trade quarterly
- Trades are unlimited
- Not taxed on gains
- Gains not reported to the IRS.
- Rules to break

Want to afford anything? Let me show you how.

You Decide.

NDA is required because this process is specialized knowledge and not for everyone.

For more information, visit:
https://www.creditcardtrading.com

Chapter 32

Credit Card Trading Course
Sneak Peek

What you will learn in the course

- How to recycle credit with no money;
- How to use powerful financial tools;
- How to get money to do business, not do business to get money;
- How to get access to 0% funding and 0% credit cards;
- How to get access to balance transfers with no balance transfer fees.

Bonus:

- Person stacking
- How to prevent generational poverty
- How to build generational wealth
- How to own nothing but control everything
- How to use OPM

Credit Card Trading Course Bonus Sneak Peek

- The forbidden spiritual science of credit only the elites know;
- What you didn't learn in school;
- The truth about banks;
- How to rob the banks legally;
- How to monetize yourself with or without money.

Visit

www.creditcardtrading.com

Chapter 33

The Unknown Truth Behind the Opening & Closing Stock.

An opening stock is an asset. It is the value of a person's life force.

A person's opening stock is the inventory of the United States Cooperation (a Business) at the start of a child's birth, once the birth certificate is created.

A closing stock is a liability.

A closing stock is the end of a person's life, the inventory of the United States Corporation loss, once the death certificate is created.

For Educational Purposes Only

Department of State Division of Incorporation registry for a Business Entity

Found on Google

Chapter 34
Closing Remarks

Wealth is achieved by having access to powerful financial tools, having an abundance mindset, and letting go of the fear of investing.

Once you align with your desired financial reality, you will unlock the door to financial freedom.

For assurance, practice saying affirmations out loud to guide you on your financial path.

Words are powerful, words can create or destroy, so use your words wisely.

When it comes to my finances, I will take a leap of faith. I will get out of my comfort zone by learning how to think outside the box.

I will test all things. If, at first, I don't succeed, I will keep searching until I find the right financial strategy that works best for me.

If my finances aren't where I want them to be, I will invest in financial education, educate myself or hire a financial coach to get faster results.

If I keep doing the same thing over and over again and not getting any financial results, it's called denial.

I will explore different financial avenues until I succeed in reaching my financial goals.

I will write down all my financial goals, starting with a budget. By doing this, it will breathe life into my financial future.

I will take my finances to the next level after I write it, read it, know it and feel it to be true because my financial thoughts are emotionally charged.

I will place my order in life, and G❤️D will cause it to be... Make it a reality.

Chapter 35
Bulletproofing Your Financial IQ

Mastering Financial Literacy

1. Understand powerful financial instruments.
2. Learn budgeting, saving and investing.
3. Grasp tax planning and optimization.

Building Multiple Income Streams

1. Diversify investments (credit stocks, real estate, etc.).
2. Develop side hustles or entrepreneurship.
3. Create passive income sources.

Protecting Your Wealth

1. Insurance planning (Infinite, life, health, etc.).
2. Estate planning and asset protection.
3. Tax-efficient strategies.

Investing Strategically

1. Understand risk management.
2. Leverage compound interest.
3. Diversify your portfolio.

Optimizing Financial Tools

1. Utilize tax-advantaged accounts.
2. Leverage powerful financial tools.
3. Streamline expense tracking.

Cultivating Financial Discipline

1. Set clear financial goals.
2. Prioritize needs over wants.
3. Avoid impulse purchases.

Staying Informed

1. Follow financial news and trends.
2. Attend workshops and webinars.
3. Read financial literature.

Networking

1. Connect with financial experts.
2. Join financial communities.
3. Seek mentorship.

Legally Maximizing Wealth

1. Understand tax laws and loopholes.
2. Utilize tax-deferred accounts.
3. Leverage legal investment strategies.

Some recommended books to get you started:

1. "The Intelligent Investor" by Ben Graham
2. "Rich Dad Poor Dad" by Robert Kiyosaki
3. "Your Money or Your Life" by Vicki Robin and Joe Dominguez

Consult financial experts and conduct thorough research before making decisions.

Chapter 36

What is a Trust

A trust is a legal arrangement where one party (the grantor or settlor) transfers assets to another party (the trustee) to manage for the benefit of a third party (the beneficiary).

Key Elements:

1. *Grantor/Settlor*: The person who creates the trust and transfers assets into it.
2. *Trustee*: The person or organization responsible for managing the trust assets and making decisions about their distribution.
3. *Beneficiary*: The person or organization that benefits from the trust assets.
4. *Trust Assets*: The properties, investments, or other assets transferred into the trust.

Types of Trusts:

1. *Revocable Trust*: Can be changed or terminated by the grantor during their lifetime.
2. *Irrevocable Trust*: Cannot be changed or terminated once it's created.
3. *Living Trust*: Created during the grantor's lifetime, often to avoid probate.
4. *Testamentary Trust*: Created through a will, taking effect after the grantor's death.
5. *Special Needs Trust*: Designed for beneficiaries with disabilities to preserve government benefits.
6. *Charitable Trust*: Benefits a charitable organization or cause.

Purposes of Trusts:

1. *Estate Planning*: Manage and distribute assets after death.
2. *Tax Planning*: Minimize taxes and optimize wealth transfer.
3. *Asset Protection*: Safeguard assets from creditors or lawsuits.
4. *Beneficiary Support*: Provide for loved ones with special needs or financial challenges.
5. *Philanthropy*: Support charitable causes or organizations.

Trusts can be complex, so it's essential to consult with a qualified attorney or financial advisor to determine the best approach for your specific situation.

Chapter 37

Pros and Cons of a Trust

Pros:

1. *Avoid Probate*: Trusts can bypass probate, saving time and money and maintaining privacy.
2. *Tax Benefits*: Trusts can minimize taxes, optimize wealth transfer, and reduce estate tax liabilities.
3. *Asset Protection*: Trusts can safeguard assets from creditors, lawsuits, and financial risks.
4. *Flexibility*: Trusts can be customized to meet specific needs, goals, and circumstances.
5. *Control*: Trusts allow grantors to maintain control over asset distribution and management.
6. *Privacy*: Trusts can maintain confidentiality and anonymity for beneficiaries and assets.
7. *Special Needs Planning*: Trusts can provide for loved ones with special needs without jeopardizing government benefits.

8. *Charitable Giving*: Trusts can facilitate philanthropic giving and support favorite causes.

Cons:

1. *Complexity*: Trusts can be intricate and require professional expertise to establish and manage.
2. *Cost*: Creating and maintaining a trust can involve significant upfront and ongoing costs.
3. *Inflexibility*: Once established, trusts can be difficult to modify or terminate.
4. *Tax Implications*: Trusts can have unintended tax consequences if not properly structured.
5. *Administrative Burden*: Trusts require ongoing administration, record-keeping, and compliance.
6. *Risk of Litigation*: Trusts can be vulnerable to disputes and litigation among beneficiaries or with external parties.
7. *Public Record*: Depending on the type of trust, some information may become public record.
8. *Grantor's Loss of Control*: Once assets are transferred to a trust, the grantor may relinquish some control over those assets.

It's essential to consult with a qualified attorney or financial advisor to determine whether a trust is suitable for your specific situation and goals.

Chapter 38

How to Set Up a Trust

Setting up a trust involves several steps, which I'll outline below. Please note that it's recommended to consult with an attorney or financial advisor to ensure your trust is properly established and tailored to your specific needs.

Step 1: Determine the Type of Trust:

1. *Identify your goals*: Estate planning, tax planning, asset protection, or philanthropy?
2. *Choose a trust type*: Revocable, irrevocable, living, testamentary, special needs, or charitable trust?

Step 2: Gather Essential Documents:

1. *Identification*: Driver's license, passport, or
    state ID.
2. *Social Security number*: For tax purposes.
3. *Asset documentation*: Deeds, titles, account
    statements, and other proof of ownership.

Step 3: Appoint a Trustee:

1. *Choose a trustee*: Individual, corporate, or
    professional trustee.
2. *Consider successor trustees*: In case the
    primary trustee is unable to serve.

Step 4: Fund the Trust:

1. *Transfer assets*: Move assets into the trust,
    such as real estate, investments, or bank
    accounts.
2. *Consider tax implications*: Consult with a tax
    professional to minimize tax liabilities.

Step 5: Create the Trust Agreement:

1. *Work with an attorney*: Draft a trust agreement
    that outlines the terms, conditions, and
    distribution of assets.
2. *Sign and notarize*: Execute the trust agreement
    in the presence of a notary public.

Step 6: Register the Trust (Optional):

1. *Check state requirements*: Some states require trusts to be registered.
2. *File with the state*: If required, file the trust agreement with the state and obtain any necessary certifications.

Step 7: Maintain and Update the Trust:

1. *Review and update*: Periodically review the trust agreement and update as needed.
2. *File tax returns*: Ensure the trust files tax returns and reports as required.

Chapter 39
What is a Financial Mindset

A healthy financial mindset is a mental attitude and approach to managing finances that promotes financial well-being, stability, and success. Here are some key characteristics of a healthy financial mindset:

1. Financial Literacy:

Understanding basic financial concepts, such as budgeting, saving, investing, and managing debt.

2. Clear Financial Goals:

Having specific, measurable, achievable, relevant, and time-bound (SMART) financial objectives, such as saving for retirement or paying off debt.

. . .

3. Positive Money Mindset:

Viewing money as a tool for achieving financial freedom rather than a source of stress or anxiety.

4. Long-Term Perspective:

Focusing on long-term financial goals rather than seeking short-term gains or instant gratification.

5. Risk Management:

Understanding and managing financial risks, such as investing in a diversified portfolio or having adequate insurance coverage.

6. Flexibility and Adaptability:

Being able to adjust financial plans and strategies in response to changing circumstances, such as job loss or market fluctuations.

7. Financial Resilience:

Having a financial safety net, such as an emergency fund, to weather financial storms and unexpected expenses.

. . .

8. Avoidance of Lifestyle Creep:

Resisting the temptation to inflate lifestyle expenses as income increases and instead directing excess funds towards savings, investments, or debt repayment.

9. Gratitude and Appreciation:

Practicing gratitude for financial blessings and appreciating the value of money rather than taking it for granted.

10. Continuous Learning:

Committing to ongoing financial education and staying informed about personal finance, investing, and money management.

By cultivating a healthy financial mindset, individuals can make informed financial decisions, achieve financial stability, and build long-term wealth.

Chapter 40

The Pros and Cons of Having a Healthy Financial Mindset:

Pros:

1. *Improved financial decision-making*: A healthy financial mindset enables you to make informed, intentional financial decisions.
2. *Reduced financial stress*: By managing finances effectively, you'll experience reduced financial stress and anxiety.
3. *Increased savings and investments*: A healthy financial mindset promotes saving, investing, and building wealth.
4. *Better financial resilience*: You'll be more equipped to handle financial setbacks, such as job loss or unexpected expenses.
5. *Enhanced financial confidence*: A healthy financial mindset fosters confidence in your financial abilities and decision-making.

6. *Improved relationships*: By managing finances effectively, you'll reduce conflicts with partners, family, and friends.
7. *Increased financial flexibility*: A healthy financial mindset provides the freedom to pursue opportunities, travel, or retire early.
8. *Better work-life balance*: By managing finances effectively, you'll have more time and energy for personal and professional pursuits.

Cons

1. *Initial discomfort*: Developing a healthy financial mindset may require confronting uncomfortable financial realities.
2. *Time and effort*: Creating and maintaining a healthy financial mindset requires ongoing effort and dedication.
3. *Potential for obsession*: An overemphasis on financial management can lead to an unhealthy obsession with money.
4. *Limited financial knowledge*: A lack of financial knowledge or expertise can hinder the development of a healthy financial mindset.
5. *Emotional challenges*: Managing finances effectively can be emotionally challenging, particularly when dealing with debt, financial setbacks, or market volatility.

6. *Potential for burnout*: Overemphasizing financial management can lead to burnout, particularly if you're shouldering the responsibility alone.
7. *Limited support*: A lack of support from family, friends, or a financial community can make it more challenging to maintain a healthy financial mindset.
8. *Continuous learning*: A healthy financial mindset requires ongoing learning and adaptation to changing financial circumstances and markets.

Chapter 41

How to set up a healthy financial mindset:

Assess Your Current Mindset

1. *Reflect on your financial values*: What matters most to you about money?
2. *Identify your financial goals*: What do you want to achieve with your finances?
3. *Recognize your financial stressors*: What causes you financial anxiety or stress?

Challenge Limiting Beliefs

1. *Notice negative self-talk*: Pay attention to negative thoughts about money or your financial abilities.
2. *Challenge assumptions*: Ask yourself if

negative thoughts are based on facts or just
assumptions.
3. *Replace limiting beliefs*: Replace negative
thoughts with positive, empowering ones.

Cultivate a Growth Mindset

1. *Embrace lifelong learning*: Commit to
continuously learning about personal finance
and wealth-building strategies.
2. *View failures as opportunities*: See financial
setbacks as chances to learn and grow.
3. *Focus on progress, not perfection*: Celebrate
small wins and acknowledge progress toward
your financial goals.

Develop a Positive Relationship with Money

1. *Practice gratitude*: Reflect on the things you're
thankful for, including financial blessings.
2. *Reframe money as a tool*: View money as a
means to achieve your goals and improve your
life.
3. *Cultivate a sense of abundance*: Focus on the
abundance in your life rather than scarcity.

Set Healthy Financial Habits

1. *Create a budget*: Establish a realistic budget that aligns with your financial goals.
2. *Prioritize needs over wants*: Distinguish between essential expenses and discretionary spending.
3. *Automate savings and investments*: Set up automatic transfers to your savings and investment accounts.

Surround Yourself with Positive Influences

1. *Seek supportive relationships*: Surround yourself with people who support and encourage your financial goals.
2. *Follow financial experts*: Learn from reputable financial experts and thought leaders.
3. *Join a financial community*: Connect with others who share your financial goals and values.

By following these steps, you can set up a healthy financial mindset that will help you achieve your financial goals and build a more secure financial future.

Chapter 42

Financial Food for Thought

I am what I eat, but I Become what I think.

I will be the architect of my Mind.

I am my greatest asset.

Knowledge is not power unless I do something with it.

When life throws me lemons, I will turn it into lemonade.

I will take action to improve my finances.

I will not be my worst enemy when it comes to finances.

I will change my mindset in order to change my finances.

I will stop standing in my own way and buy my way out of poverty with knowledge and new skills.

I will invest in myself because it pays the best dividends.

I will learn first, then earn because the more I know, the more I will earn.

I will purchase assets that put money into my pocket, not liabilities that take money out of my pocket.

The more I invest, the more I will receive financially.

I must invest money to grow money.

Anything that saves me time is a true purchase.

Bad debt is slavery. I will buy back my freedom by paying off my bad debt with different financial tools.

If, at first, I don't succeed, I will get a Financial Strategy Coach.

The poor work hard for money and focus on labor-intensive efforts.

The rich work smart for money, leveraging intelligence, strategy, and efficiency.

The wealthy emphasize long-term vision, legacy and sustainable growth.

My end goal is to make money work for me while I am awake and asleep.

INVEST IN YOURSELF

Chapter 43

Financial Encouragement

EMPOWERMENT

1. Taking control of my finances is the first step towards achieving financial freedom.
2. I have the power to create a brighter financial future.
3. Financial literacy is the key to unlocking my economic potential.

MOTIVATION

1. Every dollar saved, every debt paid off, and every investment made brings me closer to my goals.
2. I know I have the ability to manage my finances effectively.
3. Small steps today, a secure tomorrow.

CONFIDENCE

1. I got this! Mastering financial literacy takes time, but I am capable.
2. My financial decisions matter; I will own them with confidence.
3. Financial knowledge is power; I will use it to build a better life.

RESILIENCE

1. Setbacks happen, but I will not give up. I will Learn from it and move forward.
2. Financial mistakes are opportunities for growth.
3. Stay focused, stay disciplined, and stay committed to your financial goals.

INSPIRATION

1. Imagine the freedom to pursue my passions without financial stress.
2. A financially literate me is a force to be reckoned with.
3. My financial future is brighter than I think.

ACTION

1. Start small, start now. Every step counts.
2. I will take ownership of my financial education.
3. I will make today the day I take control of my finances.

Mastering my Finances is True Power. If I Change my Financial Frequency, I Change my Financial Reality.

Chapter 44
Resources/Credit

G❤️D's Holy Spirit
Alux
Nero Knowledge
Derrick Whitehead
Robert Kiyosaki
Meta AI
Google

Anyone else I forgot to mention.

Testimonials

Jeffrey:

"I have always been impressed by **Quinn's** sharp mind and practical approach to life. Truly impactful. **Quinn** has a unique ability to break down complex financial concepts into simple, easy-to-understand terms. With her guidance, I've been able to take control of my finances and make smarter decisions about my future."

I highly recommend **Quinn.** She's not only knowledgeable and experienced, but she's also passionate about helping others succeed.

Archie:

I've known **Quinn** Harris for over 25 Years. She is a dynamic and highly impactful person when it comes to personal development. She has spent most of her time helping people succeed in finance. Her professionalism and mastery of difficult financial concepts made her a sought-after person in the financial and credit card industry. She has developed a system of credit card trading that allows anyone who becomes part of her program the opportunity to become financially independent and able to understand the inner workings of finance. **Quinn** Harris Takes Complex financial concepts and explains them in an easy-to-understand manner, guiding at every turn in the learning process. I have gained valuable information that has made my financial life easier to manage and put more than just food on the table, but a future with fewer worries. **Quinn** Harris's program is designed for each person's needs. Her caring attitude, honesty, and focus on your success will help you develop smart decisions, paving the way for a bright future. I am a Tax Accountant who has been in the financial industry for over 55 years, and I give my highest recommendation to **Quinn** Harris. Let her be your mentor and guide in learning the most important ways to navigate the financial markets. Intelligence, perseverance, through determination to finish what you start are an integrated element in her program that will give you an honest real- real-life personal power to be successful.

Derrick:

"I recently had the pleasure of working with **Quinn** Harris, a true expert in credit card assistance, and I couldn't be more grateful for her help. From the very start, **Quinn** approached my financial situation with a professional and caring attitude that immediately put me at ease. She took the time to understand my needs and offered practical, tailored solutions that made a real difference. Her knowledge and dedication were evident at every step, and I'm so thankful for her guidance. Thanks to **Quinn**, I feel much more secure and confident in managing my finances. I highly recommend her to anyone seeking trustworthy, expert financial assistance!"

Author BIO

Quinn Harris is a prolific author in Business and Economics, Personal Finance and Investing, with a keen eye for financial strategies. Quinn's mission is to increase your financial IQ, to get you to work smarter, not harder, and to elevate you and your finances to the next level so you can accomplish Financial Freedom.

"Quinn's mission is to empower your financial future by:

1. Elevating your financial IQ through education and awareness.
2. Teaching you smart strategies to maximize your wealth.
3. Guiding you to work smarter, not harder, and achieve financial efficiency.

Together, let's unlock your financial potential and reach the next level of prosperity, securing your path to:

- Financial Freedom
- Peace of Mind
- Long-term Security

Quinn is committed to helping you:

- Break free from bad debt.
- Build sustainable wealth
- Create a Legacy
- Live life on your terms

Join Quinn on this transformative journey to financial freedom.